Thank you, Reagan — Cheers!

— Greg

someone used to live here, long ago

greg rudolph

someone used to live here, long ago

greg rudolph

This book is dedicated to all
those who have died and to all
those who have survived.

"if you see anything horrible
don't cling to it
if you see anything beautiful
don't cling to it."

-unknown Nepalese
lady-saint (as reported
by Allen Ginsberg)

—

a man struts in with drawn weapons—looking like an angry Saddhu. long dirty beard and crisp orange shirt. enshrined to the goddesses of India— filthy prostitute goddesses. he paces slowly in prayer to his Ego, his Elohim—woman with him, looks like someone I knew in my youth, but shorter—more plump. a glow to her skin and a love for life well lived. she scoffs at his rich devout air—with the patient mode of discipline confined to the spaces of the servants. assalaamu alaikum to you both, peace of Allah grace your heads and your hearts and your tired hands. my name is hope and I live indoors.

—

Chewing softly
Dendron petals;
Three feet up
Scurry field mice, poisoned
Chewing sugar cookie crumbs,
Not meant for childrens' supper plates.
The basil
Out front didn't grow this year,
I chew
Dendron petals, three feet up
Under my
Cedar overhang.

Safe in the burrow back home,
Field mice share crumbs with loved ones—
Wicked beasts below basil roots,
My basil won't grow.
I chew
Dendron petals
Six feet up.

The children play in the yard.
School will be back in soon
And I
Will retreat to my garage
Where no sprouts or field mice brave the cold and cracking
concrete.
In November I will
Be safe,
And I will chew
Pencils, marked with names of shops.
Auto shops.

Until sunlight fades,
I will
Chew dendron petals
Three feet up,
And slowly forget.

someone used to live here, long ago

—

there is something
in the night
with grey skin
and long horrible eyes like
burnt eucalyptus

there is no shade
of green that we
have not seen from
beneath the paling echoes
of our parents' marriage

—

Someone used to live here, long ago
Been standing empty now for some years
I remember once, a garden
out back, with creaky palisades and
iron uprights like war hardened charcoal
soldiers in twos and fours
the whole loam
overflowed with lilacs and chrysanthemums
And a gentle soul to tend it;
kept the shudders swept
And the piping clear

I remember one October afternoon
walking home from school, we heard the news—
in the bathroom on the second floor
The old man shot himself.
Left the screen door open,
slapping its frame in the wind

Now there is no garden
No one will buy the plot.

—

When you hit your low, there is a moment of clarity.

It doesn't take much to recognize. Like the smell of smoke from two houses down. Colonel burning leaves on the first day of autumn like he always has and always will.

It's naked and transparent; glass crumbling around your fist barreling through the front porch window. Your brother is at it again and your temper is blown away with the rocks sliding down from the railroad, you tipped your bike too far this time; it's a long walk home.

When you hit your low, you stand straight. Go back to the party, your shirt isn't buttoned right. You smile and someone snaps a picture.

When you lose a piece of you, the rest doesn't rock back to center. It teeters and tips along the edge of the thread pulled tight from the sleeve of your worn sweater. The fabric tears and you take it to Goodwill to be salvaged by some other sad twenty-some. When the piece that's important goes away, the frame is left to float, and no matter which way the current pulls, landfall sails further and further away.

When you hit your low, there is no sound. Plates crash and mirrors shatter and rocks tumble down. Find the biggest stone of the bunch and toss it to the stream. Your brother will catch it.

—

Who would inhabit this space,

I don't want to know until you want me to—

dare I not speak its name,

dare I not give credence to the hole that lives there:

one thousand small knees,

one thousand small feet,

one thousand small brushes to form one thousand small

strokes.

It steps in rhythm, breathes not but fumes

always

viscous smog,

every breathing thing a

conspirator and victim

one and the same; who

dares to claim a difference

———

There's a couple sitting next to me in this coffee shop. Archetypical older
white folk, this state is built on modest model citizens like this. They've been
waiting for their food for much too long. They sit and fidget uncomfortably;
I can see them in my peripherals. I've been watching them closely. I'm sure
they've been watching me too. The woman is in a grey pullover poncho. The
man in a clean button up. Middle-class modest effort. They dressed up for
this.

It's a Sunday afternoon and they're out to enjoy each other's company. The
homestead is too quiet since the kids all moved out. They can't bear to be in
silence anymore, that's why they've come to a coffee shop full of noisy youth
clacking away at their keyboards and laughing together and holding hands
and sipping their cappuccinos and waving their arms in exasperated I-told-
you-so's and surprised I-was-just-with-so-and-so's.

But they've been waiting for their food too long. The silence between them
is unbearable. It sounds like lonely separation. The boy at the table next to
them is clacking away, clacking away, and they are sitting waiting for their
food. Did the staff forget about them? Soup and salad can't take this long,
it's not right to make your customers wait like this. The shop is a ruckus
of rambunctious youth and the silence here is a brick on the table between
them.

They twiddle their thumbs, fidget with their coats. The woman leans in to ask
about the man's work. The man rolls his shoulders in exhausted explanation.
They discuss the trip they took to South America years ago. Those were good
times. Would have been much more fun without the kids. They agree and
look about for their food again, again, again. How long has it been?

I glance around me and stretch my arms, take a sip of my coffee. I meet eyes with the woman as they glance around again for their salad and soup. We both look away awkwardly, aware of each other's awareness. He touches her arm and she rubs her hands together under the table.

The shop is cold, couldn't the staff turn the thermostat up a few degrees? She says to the man, "it's cold in here, couldn't they turn it up a little?" He shrugs and she does too. The boy at the register has a hat that says "gloom" in a goofy typeface. Could he really be that upset? He was probably still a child during the housing market collapse. Much too young to remember even Desert Storm, let alone Kosovo or Vietnam. He's never had to make the hard choice of going away to serve his country and take a stand for freedom, he's only ever known safety and peace of mind. He's never known economic crisis or war or true domestic discomfort. Not like the couple next to me has. The man still has Vietnam in his eyes in the nighttime. Not the jungle, but the timberline, of course. He was only seventeen in the final year of Vietnam but he was hard at work for his father's lumber company. He still remembers the splinters in his palms. He looks to his wife for comfort. She looks around for her salad. He looks around for his soup again, again, again. She was right, it is cold in here. How long has it been?

Finally, a girl in a shirt that says 'Mill Stream Brewing' brings the soup and salad. She's not wearing a bra and doesn't apologize for the wait. The couple forgot to grab silverware or maybe assumed the staff would bring some with the meal so the woman says she'll be right back. She takes a trip to the bathroom to adjust her hair before returning with cutlery. The man thanks the woman as she returns to her seat and he straightens his back. They've been waiting much too long for this meal, his stomach pangs in his gut as he takes his first spoonful of soup. It's too hot and burns his mouth so he adjusts his shirt and waits a bit.

The food they waited so long for is gone now and they look around again, again, again for a bus tub. He asks her if maybe the staff busses the tables but she says she doesn't think so. She says she thinks she saw tubs under the station with milk and cream. They put on their jackets and she grabs her purse. He puts her plate on his and they stand to bus their own tables. They leave but forget the bowl of corn chips that came as a side to the salad. I am still sitting at the table next to where they were; clacking, clacking, clacking away. I can't bear to think of the separation in their silence. This country is built on modest model citizens like them. Like my parents, like my dead uncle, like my old boss who hates his ex-wife but loves the business they own together. Like the bowl of stale corn chips that they forgot and left behind. How long has it been?

—

It seems so nice from afar
So soft, gentle. The second snow in January—
Already the snowplows have carved through the frozen world
Divided and subdivided partitions for the ant colony; still in uneasy
slumber

Yesterday, a cloud rolled over top of
Thunderhead Peak and painted every pine with a pale champagne
In buzzing sleep cycles the mountainous circuitry shuttered
Back and forth from Santa Fe to the twin circles
"Those memories were never mine to have",
I shouted but the birds perched on the lamp post
Outside just scattered around the neighborhood

—it wasn't yesterday, I just remember it as such
Haze creeps indefinitely and dusts and powders and coats and
conceals
Many tiny glass needles
It seemed so nice from afar
Now I don't know where I am
Nothing feels right.

someone used to live here, long ago

—

On the side of the street
There is
A mint green truck
It hasn't moved in months
At least, not as far as I've seen

During hurricane season
It might
Bend back and forth
Rip and tear like paper in the grip of a child
As god might say
Goodness, how you all play like children play
Is not Gilgamesh made of the same dust and clay
As rabbits and foxes and rail cars
And does not your big green truck rust away
After my waves bend and break as a child at play
My brother, my one and only, the whole earth groans for you.

—

—

Wine drunk at 8:30
beer drunk at 10:30
sitting there alone in your extra large Jane Doe t-shirt
You sleep with the windows open even though
you won't be able to breathe come morning
Everyone wants to believe that their experience is unique
but I know you remember standing on
the shakey tram in Prague
and thinking
This might be the last time
I know her how she is
and then
Two months later, the love of your life
is sending you
midnight messages while you're
catching a bus over to
Termini to catch an
early train out to
who fucking cares where
Wine drunk 8:03, clean the
kitchen, spray down the plants
preheat the oven she's
not coming home tonight
not because she doesn't
love you—
She doesn't like you
Life got in the way
as it does

sometimes people leave and we don't know why.

—

words spoken with rushing blood
can be the most carelessly fired arrows

—

I peeled off a scab on my shin and now
there is blood on my pants so I shoved
a crumpled paper towel into my sock
and I'll soon toss it out to the dump
for someone to sift through for
minimum wage
My parents never taught me about
god but to be fair I never asked either
I guess it doesn't matter now that
I learned about god from people
who are terrified of it

—

I fell in love with a sunset once. Endlessly fascinating and beautiful and I told it so every night while it was away. Every day it waited another minute longer to show its face until winter came and the overcast grey took its place.
I fell in love with an earthquake once. It shook me like prairie grass in a dust bowl windstorm; horribly lonely, horribly afraid.
I fell in love with a dead satellite, drifting ceaselessly. Belonging only to the cold push-pull of gravity and open, endless space.

I rinsed my mouth in the kitchen sink last Tuesday and with my careless mouthwash, flushed two courageous ants down, down, deeper, down, down, the drain.

someone used to live here, long ago

—

Give patience and persistence
Give clarity and truth and accept no pittance
Live boldly and carry each sorrow as a gift
Love as severe as our time here will allow.

If misery could speak, it would impart only a single sober wisdom;
To live and to love and to never recover.

—

The time spent
lodged in between seasons
when the sun is cold
but patient still;
a master of delayed gratification
Pale blue
and lethargic
The earth travels with me
clinging to my work boots
in clumps of sodden agony.
I,
prod along, all the way to New Mexico.
The sun is warmer there
and the sand feels like a certain set of teeth;
I haven't heard scraping like this,
Not in years.

—

Check the for sale sign on your '72 Scout that you promised
to your son but now he lives upstate and your wheelchair
won't fit behind the bench seat; what does it mean when a
train crashes on the same day that a plane crashes and the
ferns where the naked innocents play burn under twisted
aluminum and the scrap yard's books finally show profits.
What does it mean when a gull makes nest on a ship bound
for beyond, never to make port again on native shores where
grows ferns and fathers and sons and mothers and hate
between lovers, what does it mean when god doesn't show;

—

The claw foot bathtub sunk into the hillside full of ash and
refuse from landscaping the wooded half-acre. The mud
covered Trooper in the driveway with duct tape sealing the
windshield. The ivy ripping into the seams of the rotting
wood flesh of the chicken coop that never could keep the
coyotes at bay. The elk down the lane, howling into the soft
moonlight that only danced once on your pale skin before
sunlight burned the haze from my balcony where I first
learned the way the world ends. The journal that I kept with
clippings and nick nacks from across Europe. The river-
polished stone that I tossed away this morning. T-shirts.
Books. Hair ties. Blankets.
Coffee mugs.
Flowers in compasses, blades of Roman grass,
notes, letters, love poems.

None of these memories mean a thing to me anymore.

—

Moving onward, onward
my father used to say
pity not the aching feet
I used to
smoke often but never habitually
I used to
cook for my grandmother
but I haven't seen her in years
and I doubt she'd recognize me now.

On a pedestrian bridge in Germany
a stranger asked for a light
and I pretended not to hear.
Habits of Roman decorum,
you know how it goes.

Begging, taking, always begging,
I could see
Palatine from my doorstep
but I don't feel like walking today.
I could smell
Lilacs and eucalyptus,
warm pollen and butterscotch wheat fields,
West Kansas was kind like that.
And if I think too hard about it
I almost want to stay here for just a little while.
Go see if Dudley Jay can spare a nine,
or a couple of cigarettes for free.
I don't have any money today.

—

I met my wife in the summertime
in Telluride,
where ponderosas scoff at the birch trees,
and where lodgepole pines catch plagues
just in time to escape an eager child's imagination
What a wonderland
What an adventure
to be afraid
and to not know why.
To be in suffering
and ache for reprieve, in the summertime
I walked with her, side stepping
Questions rising from grains
of uncooked rice
By fireside, I
smell you still, like
laundry, heaped on the floor
In the summertime, I
Wept
By the pines
for no more hazy mornings.
In saltless waves
without salted teeth
and an unconscious grin
I wish now for no Telluride, no
Jackson Hole,
Palatine divorced Aventine—
in my
fever dreams.

I am unmarried

Have been for some time now

And in my old wisdom, I

plan to retire to

Vietnam

And I will open a shop there

What glory,

to be afraid

and to not know why.

someone used to live here, long ago

—

Sometimes
when the wind is too high
Out of reach, I mean
high above our heads
and in waiting, down below
we blow into our hands to give movement
sometimes,
my eyes close like garden gates
on my flush, heirloom face
sometimes,
memories are
tool sheds with padlocked doors,
painted yellow with chips from stray baseball hits

other times,

memories are

overgrown sidewalks with stains from

where knuckles raked skin from bone—

I still know the smell of the red clay earth

in Manassas after a fresh spring rain

and I know the taste of sunlight

and the heat of sweat in dark spaces

But sometimes,

when the wind is too high

I forget how cold my skin must be

for a field of daisies to wilt

when I lay my head on its breast

and blow movement into my hands.

someone used to live here, long ago

—

Disappear from each other
As you do;
I can't bear to think of it any other way.
After all, that is the nature of things
to leave, to die, to be gone with the slow dredge of time
ripping, grinding, devouring dirt and clay
I am
anti-flesh
anti-bone
it is in my nature, as I say.
Like a bullet screeching over dirt
tilled and planted but ever without fruit,
it ricochets from bark and limb
and ebbs quietly to the brush—
there is a stream there,
runoff mostly
but gentle and persistent
and a small, earthen overwalk
shells and feathers and the like strewn about.
After a hushed summertime rain,
you can still feel the imprints of old footsteps
long since faded from thought.

I am present there still,

flesh against flesh

bone against bone

the crack of gunfire and pungent fog

looming heavy in swells like

breath from a dying fawn.

and in longing, become contra

To be absence—

a dense and ponderous wretch.

That is,

after all,

the nature of things.

—

In a whisper
found out back
between chain links
Muddy, groggy, breathing heavy;
heaving really
Shot twice, and wandered for miles
Trailing a crimson candy trail
"You're not fooling anyone"
the chain links call out to the wind
as if to expect a response
or proof of purchase—
I could smell
Blood, from my bathroom
under my nails;
in my teeth.
Heaving, heaving
out back in the mud
Rising, falling gut split open
Heaving
As the wind blows.

—

Two miles to the Northeast, just across the river
they prefer kilometers but I don't know the
exact measurements
Kindly tended hills littered with crescent moons and
Eastern crosses
There is no entry fee but they suggest donations
Sessioned among small bricks and busts of
Mary and Jesus
creeps an obsidian pyramid
Gaudy and incongruous
and downslope,
submerged in reeds and unruly sod
a monument.
Not large—
etched with but eight words:

Arrogant. Ultimately, horrid and incorrigible.
He died alone.

—

I rolled pipe smoke back and forth
in the alley out of boredom
shop owner asked if I'd like to
partake in his ganja ritual,
I obliged
just underneath the tepid ballroom
out of use for a decade or so
there was a murder
out where I left my ash and litter
another young girl taken by the hatred of male sexuality
and another
stained yellow dress shoved hastily into
grease dumpster, many more stains after that
glass shoes upstairs tap tap tap away in waltz
one two three, one two three lovers trip home over
one another
so she asks me, if I ever enjoy the fruits of my work and I say
no a photographer should never drink on the job
and I leave to chat more with my other current lover
and outside knelt under overhang,
young beggar prays for nickels in their wool hat but I've
never given money to charity so why start now
I trip into nearby pasticceria and purchase a beer to
smash in the street and beggar yells
in a tongue I'm only familiar with when
ordering street food and telling scam cabbies
to fuck off
why condone such haste and
restlessness
why abide
the violence of youth
in the city of god

—

A patient bee in a searching for its pollen stinging at my calf
but I dont mind I welcome the needle of mine tiny yellow
friend as it were we together make springtime it in its gentle
splendor and me in my tattered shoes and blue jeans I hear
the hum from its backbone laughing at the still air and
everywhere the call of a joyous finch just happy to be here I
sputter a loud yawn and stretch my limbs me in waiting for
the next sorrow to dwell into but grass tickle at my ankle and
the tiny violet blooms of this earths kind morning breath
give pause to mine wrinkled brow in this moment as my
good yellow friend prick and prod at mine regretful flesh.

—

be gentle

good god, be gentle

I am not

as wild, angry sea birds

crashing to shore

for victuals robbed from mollusk shells—

pearlescent like soft-talk from the sanguine

mouth of

a high school crush

I am not strong

not anymore

an early summer storm can be

such a violent thing,

be gentle

—

So curious, how quiet it all is
waiting in the sun
between chipped whitewash and the
sprinkler spat spat spatting away at
an arm outstretched from
the window of a pitch-black Ford:
to be in posture of reaching, ad nauseum—
When I was young, I
spat peas and carrots onto the floor
in stubborn protest of my parents'
failing marriage.
I vowed
to marry a beautiful woman
to father beautiful sons and daughters
to show my parents how selfish they were
to feed me peas and carrots.
When I was young, I
picked honeysuckle from the hillside
above the creek behind my house
And I swore
it was the sweetest taste any man would ever know.

Until I fell in love

And I swore

it was the sweetest taste any man would ever know.

Until my eyes got grey

and my mouth got smokey

and I learned how to hold bourbon cleanly between my

cheek and tongue

and I swore

I would never again know the taste of a honeysuckle

because the honeysuckle that grows

in the patient hills of the old Sioux

just doesn't taste the same as I remember

in the grass

on the hill

above the creek

behind my house.

—

Photos of Myself; My Grandfather, 1999

Once on a front porch, I sat,
my grandfather in a bed upstairs, he lay
Strong once, a sailor's hard skin
a submariner's iron fortitude
now frail, too many cigars or too
many failures, who's to say
Now filled with cancer, filled with
love from every room
Every outstretched palm in posture of
giving freely, grace and bearing weight
of mortality, one shoulder linked to
each other shoulder
hands and bones intertwined
To breathe is to ache
And as I pace, imagining this moment
across little monuments in patiently
manicured landscape on a
hill somewhere I don't remember, I feel
the sun between the cold clouds, holy

like a quiet oasis, a tiny old mirrored reprieve
of all animals for many miles surrounding
No wars are fought for this land
No death could touch this
quiet space And I pace again
down hill and up and I pick a dandelion for
my mother but her face is not her face
but the shadow left from something gone too soon
and we get back in the car and
drive home and I clutch the sacred
butter-yellow until sleep overtakes me.
Upstairs, my grandfather labors for
breath but outside we huddle like
a tribe of antiquity long before the
gift of Prometheus, bracing against the
cold November wind. A photo is
snapped and we all shuffle off
to sob and ache and wither away in
closets and dark kitchens. Ambling
forward with each heartbeat, o' death
what have thee made for us.

someone used to live here, long ago

—

I should like to rule the world.
Into the function of things, I would build
greenways—
long tiled stretches with clay masonry studded with
dandelions
and in the place of each street light, I would erect
cottonwood
and each white breath of my world
would contain three syllables,
bilabial passing with waltz to alveolar
a most patient and deliberate pirouette.

—

A flickering television set
betrays the visage
as night passes to grey
I should like to flip the channel away from static
but we stay unmoving still, you and I
locked inside of what balance may bring
if hands and teeth touch too far down the clock
perched heavy, on a dusk-brown
This is what danger muted yellows may bring
outpacing their own tremoring fingertips
This danger of control,
subtle, with vignetted corners
edging in, closer with each heartbeat
beat, beat
White knuckles, I
driving East, to the edge of town
there, timid among rusted steel longbars
peeling away from ancient branches
square-cut and black with tar from by-gone
New Deal enterprise—
Toss out bits of old flowers
dried and pressed. and say
Make beds and grow, you lot, and if ever you should like to speak, you
must first be pressed and dried. Your precariousness be venerated and
should violence catch your pace, you must at once be pressed and dried,
this world has no place for your folly. Plucked, pressed, and dried I have
made you and plucked, pressed, and dried you shall remain.
So it should be said
if every aluminum signal plate
be towed from loose gravel
and be made into my
steeples and masonry.
So it should be
in spring of my reign.

49

———

What can this meadow teach,
I groan in impatience as I sit
once again, without thought,
desire, or volition:
on moving forward—
I,
thumb through Ted Kooser and
absorb the sunlight.
Some days I,
am eucalyptus
drinking in my surroundings,
joyful in each displeasure.
I greet passing grins
from fawns of the human pedigree
with such delicate kindness my
mother thought wise to instill in me.
Some days I,
am torrential
ripping seam from joint
pounding pistol against skin
on the concave side of my skull.

I should like to see each
soft breath stolen from each
fawn of human pedigree.
I, horrid
should greet Ozymandias
and be each displeasure laid upon
the chest of ye, mighty.
Some days I,
sit upon stones
shaped and polished by Shoshone
in ages prior to
the Exploitations of my paternal lineage
without desire or volition,
and in light of sunshine
made in times of genesis—
I,
be made as
gentle brush,
drinking nourishment
from the green earth of mine newest nation.

someone used to live here, long ago

—

Sun hits
Leaves, dried;
trees sway
Easily.

—

There

be it as it may,

so loud I clasp my ears close 'neath my

sweating palms

Backward it may be—

strewn about as a child would throw it to the floor

Tall as a giant

and brave

brave like Daniel

but foolish as Leviathan and dug deep into hallowed ground,

the Fern King is a prideful man

Step not in his governance lest thee be invited in for dinner—

supper, as they say

'No Daisies, Hippies, or Blacks

WHITES ONLY'

I read once on a sign

posted too close to a public school, K-6

a scoop of tallow may do

and if not, many reeds fed over time

Many reeds

and add the tallow too, for good measure

—

Little homes—painted:

a study of who might live here

when purpose has left

to find happiness

out there

somewhere

How long a shadow they must cast

on graves of thoughts

in times, long before—

move

move, with my line

move, gentle, be ease, be grace, be

dew on morning greens;

How dare I

how dare I cast

such a thin, unbroken shape

HOW LONG AND TERRIBLE A SHAD_W

a bundle of grapes or a

bundle of stones

or a billboard

Selling parchment and

used souls—half price (one day only)

DEATH COMES

———

The first morning in the new world could have been a blaze. Your bed sheets could have been soot across the Sonoma Valley and the motes dusting the tip of your nose the smoke billowing like thunderheads rolling slowly back to the sea. Lightning cracking down over rolling hills of sangiovese that would never be pressed for nectar.

Your first words could have been blistering tidal hatred beating against the cliff side, an arm's length away from Death Valley's sweet salvation. You could have breathed deep as the ocean gave groan to the death of the great American West. Your hands could have been stoic mountain peaks, and your bruises, the black and blue alpenglow reigning weary settlers back to shelter.

On the first night in the new world, you drove north on I-35 and waved goodbye to the violent blue-greys of fading romance. Outside of a bus stop, a lonely beggar with bright red spiders slashing her nose asks if you can spare a cigarette to warm her lips for the empty in-between after the dead of winter and before the rebirth of spring. Ash and snow flurry past, mingling in quiet matrimony, ringing in the end of the Old World.

Markets are crashing. Airplanes are falling. California is burning. The first morning of the new world is silent and lonely as a beggar smoking a cigarette at midnight between here and Elsewhere. In the morning haze, the walls are more blue-grey than under the pressing hand of a noontime sun.

—

December 27th.

A good pour. Too good. Floral and nutty. Sweet on the front end and a gentle exposure lingering long after I put down my glass.

I keep putting down glasses.

Now I seem to have misplaced the bottle.

Or had I drained the contents?

I remember having at least half of a pour.

Where has the time gone.

August 21st.

A decent pour. Too sweet for my tastes. I'd rather the rough oak tang to balance the soft corn and wheat.

I'll put this one aside for safe keeping.

October 31st.

Salty and rough. Not for me. I thought I saw the old Green around somewhere but now I'm too drunk to remember. I think I'll think deeply on it in the morning. I'm already out clopping down the street. What good would I be digging around the house now. Good night, moon.

Good night, hands.

February 11th.

Poisoned myself again. It started off as an accident but now I'm not so sure. Can't quite remember how to tie a bowline. Guess I'll make something up. Don't know what I drank. Wasn't good. Drunk, though. Did the trick.

August 17th.

it's my birthday again. want the old Green today but I can't find the bottle anywhere. the Blue will do this year I guess. might know where to find a knife to cut the double-fisherman. think I'll go for a drive.

—

June 1st.

This nothing space, my brother calls it—fancies himself
a study of the human psyche. Locked away in his office
nothing space. Notarizing papers for medium fauna with no
faces. Here I rest in thought, in my nothing space, blending
music and speech and making my internal orchestral buzz.
Making my ocean waves and gentle salt breeze. Til' legs cross
my vision, dry legs spilling out of a sundress like oak roots
from a crumbling hillside near seashore in upper Maine. I
feel intrusive in my nothing space. I spill back to the world
of miniature, medium, and megafauna.

—

Kind souls, toss back and forth
up and down a snowy slope they play they play they play.
God has been kind to them.
Blessed this sacred journey of ours out back
to the big falling water place.
Frozen stiff in its place
don't you dare take a step off the trail
you'll be
frozen in your place too.
Bless your steps,
bless each and every one,
take several moments before you make your moves
and pray hard, children
pray hard.
Whitewashed, this bridge
blanketed in thick white
almost like fog
but soft like
soft like whispers.
I wish you could have seen it.
If you go just a little farther—

just another couple of steps,

you can see it resting.

Frozen there in its place, forever,

the big falling water place.

There are men,

braver than I,

They want to tame it.

To own it.

The great falling water place.

Another few steps,

just one more big reach.

A big stretch of the arms,

calf muscles pulling tight

one more inch and then they'll have it.

The big falling water place.

Godless men these are.

someone used to live here, long ago

—

there's a hole in the basement, the kind that goes on for
miles and miles down down further down always falling
further and further
I think the ancients put it here long before this house was
built

(-18437.67 (give or take))

they had only primitive mining tools, hatchets and shovels
and the like none of the sparkling yellow tunnellers that they
use in the coal shutes out east, kentucky ways
just pickaxes and hands
slaving away day in and day out to build this here,
this hole to go down down further down and further down
if you could fall into the hole you would not touch the
bottom, you would reach the core of the earth and you would
fall no further, but you would bob, up and down and around
with the push pull of gravity's fluctuations as the earth
around you bends and cracks

denser and looser, patch by patch, (that's the way the ocean
moves, tidal motion aside)

they say the magma hits a hundred thousand degrees, that's
a thousand, a hundred times
when I was young I counted to five thousand
and I could go no further
if you stepped into the hole you would count five thousand
feet in a matter of seconds
down here in this basement
who knows what the ancients were looking for all those years
ago, silver or gold probably—but I think it was something
darker than that, something less reflective. something like a
god, in the sodden earth and soil and when they didn't find
it six feet below they kept going and going and going until
the heat burned them all away.

—

I feel my bones move inside of me
popping and compressing like
pistons and camshafts
little sensors scattered
about to see how it's all doing
there's a little divot in my back
and my spine falls on either side
if I crick my neck just so, rocking
back and forth to feel
my own tender mechanisms
my tendons pull tight and go loose
and I observe myself like
a nervous grad student brushing and
sifting and scraping away at
the sand in Göbekli Tepe
I am an empty urn or
an old red truck that would
probably run again if you just
swapped out the alternator
and patched the oil pan
but everyone knows you
just don't have the time
even to have it towed

so it will wither away in the
sun and crack a little more
each time the basin floods
I've heard that this place used
to be a forest but that
was a long time ago now
and ages and ages and ages of
man have come and gone,
these days, you'd be hard
pressed to find any brush
that could bear to take root.
If you teeter up to the top of the hill there
with your motor and piston corpse
pulley system that yet breathes
you can still see where the waves meet
the stone faced lion guardians that hold
steady the shore line of Anatolia and
if you look South and squint your eyes
and click your fingers together just right
you'll hear the sound of the oldest god this
world has ever known, whisper so lightly, like
april breeze or the quietest little cottonwood:
go on, it's ok

—

A month from today it will be my 25th birthday and
I will find myself further from love than I have ever been—
the poor dominion of poor old fools, so
I wrote an anthem of sorts, a pledge that I'd like to see
children
forced to reconcile with their tiny wits about my words
standing in formation with their tiny red palms pressed deep
into
the tiny red place where the tiny bad things linger
It should be read as follows; I encourage you to stand at
attention with the poor poor
fools
poor poor fools:

I give now my attention and my irreconcilable little heart
to systems and symptoms
to structures that my mothers and fathers have chosen for me
I give now my peace
and I give my brevity
and I give my
sunshine
for the collective good,
we
the people offer you, oh aluminum goddess
you, polyvinyl chloride leviathan
Moscow, Kiev, Pyongyang, Riyadh, red white and blue clad
daemon called columbia
trickle down your drippings and your gristle I don't need
much
just a drop every day or two to stay

hydrated

dear motorcar in my driveway

I should like, if you'll have me

to take you to prom

and in the sticky bathroom inhale your exhaust from under your

upholstery

and in nine months we should, you and I

leave your gasoline soaked miscarriage on the doorstep

of my algebra teacher's ranch style duplex

Just children ourselves

our smooth faces and squishy crimson heart things

pounding pounding pounding away

reconcile thee! you fools, you porous willowy fools

I,

pledge

to mistreat, misinterpret, and love only at my most bare

convenience

I,

citizen of no confidence

bear no shame in the name of this land

I,

pledge

today, tomorrow, the next day, and the day after

to consume to consume to consume to consume to consume

to consume to consume to consume to consume to consume

to consume to consume to consume to consume to consume

to consume to consume to consume to consume to consume

to consume to consume to consume to consume to consume

to consume to consume to consume to consume to consume

—

On the edge of a very tall building somewhere,
        there is someone waiting
        to die a death worthy of a life
        spent waiting for too many things

Out upon the city, the lights tremble
        on-off-on, swatting away
        pestilent helicopters—or guiding their
        voyage home

Wherever you go. Wherever you find yourself
        there will be spring blooms and
        somewhere out in the middle

Waiting patiently for pollination
        will be a soft yellow-white
        with skinny outstretched legs.
        And it will remember the scent of you—always.

—

I told her I loved her and she replied—

                               what do you know
                               about love—

then she said I love you too—

                             a parcity I've never
                 claimed to understand.

what do I know about love? Some pulpy
substance issuing forth from this fleshy
pump organ. A savory drink to fill a
brownish-hand painted cup? What kettle boiled
this stew that we, fauna, spew upon each
other. And who drinks this umami brew with
good and clear mind—what intoxicating
sanguine liquor—I'd rather cheap beer.

              Who bore this necessity to consume,
Show me to their bedchamber and I'll
be the first in line to smother their
pocked and gristled face.

—

Morning - 8.18.18

Pulpy bits still swirling around
under my chest of flesh.
under my pounding crimson flesh battery

Someone texted me happy birthday
at 3:34 am . my birthday is
over you lout , you missed
the boat
for these swirly, pulpy bits to
attach and assemble into
something that makes sense

I couldn't remember how to
spell her name—could be that
I am just hung over
who's to say

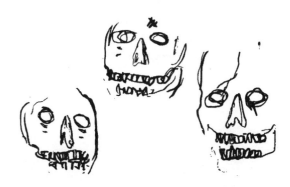

———

Do you remember the Russian
number stations? Popping
out digits at random to the
airwaves, I don't know if you
heard them or   not—you
need a HAM radio. Not many
people care for the randoms and
the unexplainables. pop pop popping away.

shest . adin . cem . dva .
chtire . adin . shest . vocem .
adin . tri . pyat . devet .

No I don't think so.
What do you think the random
pop plops do to the static of
pulpy scramble up in the head
cavity. Where do you think the
numbers go when they enter the
hearing holes. Just down the
canal, splashing off into the

brain juice splish splashing away
like some child on a beach somewhere
with—uh— big floaty bobs strapped
to their arms— a s i f , the little
fauna creatures would not still
drown if one were to
uh—crack their little shoulder bones so
that their little arm bobs would bob bob
up above their heads
uh—

devet . cem . shest . tri .
dva . dva . tri . vocem .
девять . семь . шесть . три .
два . два . три . восемь .

I don't know where this static
runs off to when my head fizzles out
and I   sleep.

—

How many bones go into building
the new corporate KG office
downtown—on the west side
How much mushy meat substance
gets chewed up for the lunch breaks
How many bolts have snapped being
driven between steel beams
what is the hex value for their
crimson Jolly Roger
        this feels overdone.

Could you believe how many chemicals
are poured into a vat to form the
silky black pavement to run
        our
hands across when we are
        feeling
lonely—but financially comfortable
        so we
buy buy buy
in repetitions of threes
can you believe the
        smell
        and
        how long it lingers down
        here

—

you've felt it too, I know you have
the restless breach punching through the
back of your skull at 4 am
the upstairs neighbors are fucking
but I hear only bed springs
the rats in the walls are fucking too
but I hear only scraping against hard plaster
and I pick at the calouses inside my
fingers I don't remember the last time
my hands felt something soft
I don't remember the last
time my breath tasted like
honesty and
patience

—

There is a fly—There was a fly
        in my room.
It poked around my earlobes as I
waited so patiently for sleep, I
flipped on the lights and traced it
through the air
twirling, twirling about
rather slowly
for a house fly.
It was
        tired probably
                like me

or near death
           maybe
                like me.
it
hovered gently over a glass on my bed
stand—left behind from hydrating a
former lover—I
slap, snapped my hand down
over the rim.
My prisoner now—this fly.
Its destiny, my charge.
        How fickle and hateful my gaze.
I flipped the rim and dunked the poor
fellow in the toilet.
        A life rescinded with a flush
how precarious.
I don't think I'll drink from that glass again.

—

the bosses went home sick and I

napped at my desk because

everyone knows I

don't sleep well

I dreamed

of an old roommate

yelling and pouting and screaming and

breathless

and I woke up sweating

still sitting behind

my computer screen

angry orange and blue flashing

back and forth between

each other

and a migrane creeps into my

upper molars

so I drive home drifting off here and there

but I keep the wheel straight because

I was a bus driver and now it is

muscle memory

not because I

want to survive the trip back

and once home I

sit down with a cup of coffee

and keeping working working working working working

—

A letter to K.:

Pillar of salt sit upright between
me and J. and
A. kept hanging around hanging onto my drunken shoulder
saying
I love you
i love you you mean so much
And in
saying so make it less so?
Sat with S.
Licking licking away
at, pillar of salt
to burn away our taste buds
Chewing cigarettes for a while
—til my sinuses ached and I could chew no more, I remember
Once
knowing the taste of someone so well
and the soft curves of the fabric pulled tight around
bones, those bones
    hard to differentiate
from my own
That salt of sweat and sometimes tears
so much like
the rich red Manassas soil caked in deep under my
fingernails and
Somewhere along the way that grit becomes
workmanship and the ultraviolet ends become
'just earning a paycheck' or 'just keeping my head busy'
And I can no longer tell one from the other

and to admit my own carelessness, I
dare not pry nor seek understanding
I know only that the sweet-salty crimson is gone;

I'll make a wager with you
that 1000 bengali goyim know better than I
The smell of delicate, familiar heat in dark
spaces and care of movement with the little
fauna in the circles surrounding;
Sweet M.: if only you could watch them dance
their little daisies, their little figs
held high above their heads
Spinning Spinning around
in prayer in
submission to their little god of clay
in love or servitude, whatever be the common vernacular
Sweet M., if you could see the coastline like
the cavernous hazel painted into the pits of this
wooden Edo face that I
dance with
on and on and on

—

thin woven lace
drips coolly down my windowsill
brave against the soot brush
pulling and ripping in slow motion
like wheat glazed over with fresh frost;
gracie galloping like a fawn, and her fat tongue
dripping with anticipation as she jack knifes
a pitiful bleeding old rabbit, too weak now to run or beg
the high sun kisses my cheek and I hear you.

a long, sleepy exhale as one dream passes for the next
I hear you but I don't speak your name
I watch the motes in slow motion, grabbing and
pulling at the aching golden sunbeams
I hear you pull closer to the pillow and I press
harder into frozen ground

ice cracks in the pockets where mud once made canyons
gracie laps at the crumbled edge of a tributary
but whines in disappointment at the hard white earth
you mumble a soft, broken phrase to your sunny
coastline dreamworld and I pull up
two bundles of snow
for gracie and me to share

———

I can smell it in the air.
there's a smoke about him.
A haze in the way he shakes your hand
and says
"real scorcher out there, huh?"
His hair is a wildfire
crackling with
deep amber waves.

why do we keep building
where the fires keep burning

Out West, there is a house
cracking backward over a cliffside
Like Dover challenged her to stay
outside, all winter long

It burned away this June
I cannot remember the color of her front porch
but I dreamed last night of one last
candlelit conversation about the shutters and bookshelves
and lace curtains and dust motes dancing in the
sunlight
and afterward,
a deranged man with a buck blade
split my gullet
outside on the concrete.

why do we keep building
where the fires keep burning

—

There's a baseball game!
gather round the park you darlings,
There's a Baseball game!
stop the frisbee throwers
lest their discus end up on the pitch
there's a Baseball Game!
Harvey and I
make circles about the park like
cotton vultures
Slinging sodas and bottled water for
a nickel above counter price
we call it a delivery fee but the
Adults won't pay—they say
Scram, you rotten boys
Up in the trees behind the Grandstand
the girls all play and
Harvey and I
scheme and conspire
to outclimb and outwit the bravest and strongest
so we may garner favor
and make good husbands to good wives but the

Girls giggle and draw their own schemes
in the dirt
they say—
Scram, you rotten boys
and over by the concession stand
atop a mound of dusty clay
the weak children too frail for the
Baseball game(!)
Make battle for the lordship of
the little clay mound
before it is
Dumped into the Real diamond
to whet the plates with fresh dust
for the Real men—squeezed into
tight grey slide pants and bright
Tiger jerseys
to usurp the earth from the weak ones
Here thee, hear thee
gather thine mitts and creaky
folding chairs
There's a baseball game!

someone used to live here, long ago

—

Brown shirts, grey shirts, blue denim
shirts, ochre flannel shirts everyone has
pulled out their autumn shirts
and pants and
hats
the air is changing here
drying out
blowing around
mixing up
the dirt
and the trash tossed in
the dirt
and my head twists around
and dawdles down
to Mexico where the
season echoes about on
harvest colors but
the air is still too hot and a
bead of moisture falls from my
brow and I ache for snow
so in twilight when

the sun doesn't see me
I twist off my
bed sheets and tug at
the red bits of the flags flapping up on poles
like scarecrows antagonizing
the flocks on their way to warmer
steppes—and I make
auburn blindfolds with which I will
wrangle the sun back into the
earth to eat up the trash
I have tossed from my
car window
from time to time.
————————

No sleep again.
        how many hours have I
lay here with eyes shut. imagining
I asleep. I miss the elk down the lane,
howling away at thunderheads. No fauna
keep better company into the delicate hours of the morning

My eyelids are sandbags I
poke around my room: so empty
So much dust piled up at the foot of
bedside lamp. How many hours
have you crept around in dead
dark of the world with me.
Have only changed the bulb once—
had thing since K. or
since I moved out or so.
I miss the elk down lane.
I. miss shapes in my wall that
twisted and morphed in post
mid-night delusions. I miss torrents
rushing off the
corner of roof and slapping at my window.
I roll over and tap at phone. another "where are you"
to pretend I didn't see.
                where am I not
                in this day and age
My eyes roll around and my beard is
uncomfortable. I flip off my light
and get up to go shave.

—

H.

How is the heat.

Do you see canyons where you live/

I saw canyons passing through lower Idaho. Not sure they look the same. Know they don't look the same. More grass in Idaho. Odd though. You poke above the canyon head. Sign says "Beware—High winds". Odd wind planes—no trees for miles around. Just prairie grass tossing about like pivoting heads atop shoulder blades of dervishes twirling away. Agoraphobic sitting up there on the edge of the world. A panic sets in that you'll never breath normal. You'll never find another word to speak to the fauna close to you. Just wind, and twirling dervish prairie grass.

Have you seen a sandstorm down there? I'd like to see a sandstorm. Have seen pictures—post-storm. Waking to a new world like the morning after raucous and shameful lovemaking—there was snow all night and when you drive her home you don't speak. You both watch the fresh earth pass and think of what life put before you that led you here. And you think of how to build a life for yourself out of the blank white earth Elohim has delivered to you in wake of your night of sin. I'd like to wake into a world fresh after a sandstorm. Press my face hard into the hot ochre drift and feel the grit tug at my skin and my hands follow the shape of canvas from dorsal to my ears to my nose to the nothing beneath.

and how red is the sky. How much do the clouds bleed into the earth when the winds calm. How does it feel to be held by the sun's bare fingers. What songs do the birds and the insects and the lizards cry in their joyous lovemaking to the new red earth.

H. I hope you are well.

Will visit soon.

—G

someone used to live here, long ago

—

It opens and it closes
        a rough duality
between beast and man
        my thoughts are shaken.

and you've the sun
        tattooed on each of your toes
building a nest like a little
        ruby hummingbird and

padding it gently
with refuse
        white powder coating
        your teeth and lips

—

Addiction took a few of my friends
and takes more still
I used to think
I could command the skies
not to grip too tightly to
wrists that were accustomed only
to razor blades and
pulled down sweatshirt sleeves
and I knew that the
holes worn in by
bleeding thumbs
where never meant to be fashion,
but protection.

I used to think
Everyone in the world was safe
under the mindful nose of my
kind mother
And in the moments she was
weeping,
the midnight blue hands
of my aunt's grandfather clock

ceased their endless march
and were quiet for a moment—
I used to think
If I was kind
and strong and
held my shoulders just right,
no one I loved would ever
go the long way away.

I used to think
the whole world would be fine
until I learned I was no
more in control than the
spinning tires on wet asphalt
in June out past t. avenue
I do not know where the wind
carries our consciousness when we
are no longer strong enough to
hold our colors inside of our flesh
I do not wish to know.
I do not know what aches us
beyond hope

or what makes us uneasy
on top of steep hills
or in very small rooms with
many unknown faces or
in the slow hours of the
morning with red and heavy eyes—
I do not wish to know.
I do not know what hides behind the
empty gaze of the escapist—
I firmly attest that I no longer wish to know.

I know that among the aching and
discomfort and addiction and aversion
and lovelessness and loneliness
there is still sunlight.

Even behind pale overcast,
no matter how overdone the metaphor,
there is still sunlight.
And I know that there are lush
fields north of Kansas where
I have lay my head and

someone used to live here, long ago

sunk into the soft prairie grass
and I have soaked long and deep
in the golden warmth of the greenest earth.
And I know that even in the tightly
clasped fist of
patiently cultivated hatred there is still the
profound and consolatory smell of wet
earth after springtime rain.

I know that all eyes close.
But all closed eyes must have once been open.

to T. C. M. A. M. & S.

—

there is smoke
            pouring from the windows
and I can hear the wood
popping and creaking in
the heat.

someone used to live here, long ago
and now in its loneliness
the earth has grown a blaze
            inside the belly
of this great ugly wolf.

Waning and waxing moon cylcles pirouette
around and around and in the underbrush
sprouts one little fern, a fig tree, a bramble of
delicate blackberries
                  no forest grows
            without violent flame
from time to time.

a c k n o w l e d g e m e n t s

—

to my friends and family. I love you all dearly. to William Bortz for inspiring me in many more ways than you know. to the Des Moines Writer's Workshop for grounding me and giving me the springboard to accomplish this piece. to my parents for their unending love and support. to every human I have ever loved passively, actively, transiently, or otherwise.

I love you still.

thank you.

Made in the USA
Columbia, SC
20 November 2018